Dreaming During the Advent of Rain

poems by

Laura Juliet Wood

Finishing Line Press
Georgetown, Kentucky

Dreaming During the Advent of Rain

Copyright © 2020 by Laura Juliet Wood
ISBN 978-1-64662-223-8 First Edition
All rights reserved under International and Pan-American Copyright Conventions. No part of this book may be reproduced in any manner whatsoever without written permission from the publisher, except in the case of brief quotations embodied in critical articles and reviews.

ACKNOWLEDGMENTS

Many thanks to the publications in which the following poems previously appeared:

West Marin Review: "Composting"
Atlanta Review: "Gloria's Café: Ventura, CA"
The Los Angeles Review: "Late Summer Garden"
The Ofi Press: "Regret"
Under the Volcano: The Best Writing of our Best Fifteen Years: "A Season for Prophecy," "Childhood Illness" and "Spring Coming"
"Their Little Room" and "Late Summer Garden" were also previously published in the chapbook, *All Hands Lost*, by Finishing Line Press, 2013.

Publisher: Leah Maines
Editor: Christen Kincaid
Cover Art: Jennifer Elzweig
Author Photo: Aislinn Kate Rehwinkel Photography/Wave Photo
Cover Design: Elizabeth Maines McCleavy

Printed in the USA on acid-free paper.
Order online: www.finishinglinepress.com
         also available on amazon.com

Author inquiries and mail orders:
Finishing Line Press
P. O. Box 1626
Georgetown, Kentucky 40324
U. S. A.

Table of Contents

In the Afterlife 1

A Season for Prophecy 2

King's Canyon 3

The Evening's Why 4

Their Little Room 5

Gloria's Café: Ventura, CA 6

Regret 7

Childhood Illness 8

We Ease into this Life and Ease out; The Rest Is Struggle ... 9

Upright of Everything 11

First Trimester 12

Second Trimester: Central Park Playground in April 13

Third Trimester: Dreaming During the Advent of Rain ... 14

What the Morning Brings 16

A Family Goes to Bed: Ventura, CA 17

Parkinson's Disease 18

A Quiet Life 19

Late Summer Garden 20

Wheeling 21

Fixed 23

Sit 24

What You Said After Your Death 25

Composting 26

Spring Coming 27

*For Caroline, Lucy and Victor
in memory of their father
John Hubbard Wood (1941-2016)*

And for angels everywhere

In the Afterlife

There are no widows, no windows of time before cancer wins. In the afterlife, you will not be diagnosed, treated, and left to wait. There will be no side effects or symptoms. In the afterlife, we will not call an ambulance every 30 days because you have stopped breathing again. We will not have to ask you to lie down. But if there is no death in the afterlife, perhaps there is no birth, and our daughter will be there, one day, as if she always had been a part of that realm. In the afterlife, I will not have to watch her lose you one evening at a time. I will not have to ask her if she wants to say goodbye to your body. Twice. Or explain to her where you went; or console the cat; or sort through your clothes. In the afterlife, there are no regrets. We will meet you there

A Season for Prophecy

The planets line up for supper. The maids are in a row.
With whom did you attend the dance at the barn?
The plate of it, the serving of the heavens as a meal.
The sin of knowing history before it happens, the ability

to tell stars from moons and the diameter of corn.
My grandmother swore she heard voices.
Weren't they these, the ones I gallop to at harvest time?
The wallpaper, too, has its tune, the antique rocker its rumba.

Swallows nest in curtains; paper flags roll off the tongue
at dusk. Those are verses that were his eyes.
And I have heard the mermaids singing, reach to reach.
When the words come, they are revelations on a fork.

When songs come, they are sung in other languages.
I taste them as though I'd licked them from a globe.

King's Canyon

There we were, crossing a bridge strung across a chasm,
King Ferns in the basin, a chatty couple fifty paces behind.

We hurried to keep our distance, preserve
the silent space. John and I

were six months away from engagement, a year
from marriage. Perhaps the other couple

thought we were sweet: a father trying
to keep up with his daughter. The rocks

were Martian red. Blood red. My future husband
suspended between prostate cancer

we were in Australia to forget
and brain cancer we didn't yet know he had.

When I remember this day, we
on the swing-bridge over the gorge,

I remember the couple as they passed us. She
in striped shirt, khakis, floppy hat. He

in baseball cap, shorts, SLR camera attached
to his hip. They looked so innocent going up

the other side of our canyon.

The Evening's Why

What drew us
to convene—

in this cactus dusk,
dusty heat?

We huddle under the market's tarp
as if it were sky.

The cloud of monarchs:
tiger-striped and tilting.

A young girl sits with her father
and shares a Coca-Cola—

the smell of coconut pomade
woven into her hair.

Mexico gave us her sand, injured
pomegranates—the white spiral of her sun—

slugs that slide across the heart, slip
beneath pots of purple basil in pairs.

Their Little Room

The bride's joy is just-watered,
fern green—
When the mouth smiles,
the heart had better smile, too.

Scorpion, melon, boot.

The moon waning, the crooked spout.
Peach blossoms are the first sign of spring.

Wrapping and unwrapping, the bride pleads,
"I want to be a window, not a door."

Everything begins with desire.
The groom walks in choreographed silence
through black water, diamonds, pine—

Their cupboard is full but soon empties.

Gloria's Café: Ventura, CA

After my husband's radiation treatment, after blood samples
for the oncologist, visits to the cardiologist, the PCP or pharmacy,
between calls to the insurance company, the credit card issuer,
the lawyers, banks and worried family members, we go
to Gloria's for food.

We sit in the same burgundy leather booth
with faux wood/really Formica tabletop
and talk cancer and talk not-talking cancer.

Our *totopos* arrive in a red basket and the salsa verde in a plastic *molcajete*.
La Virgen rests on a shelf above the grill next to a radio,
as if she, herself, were singing the rhythms that carry us home.

Our 'wet' burritos soothe something, pretend to answer questions,
rescue doubts. For the moment we forget brain cells,
stop pronouncing *glioblastoma multiforme* as though we've said it
our whole lives. We let the beans and cheese and rice and flour tortillas
in their red sauce slide into us while we stare out the huge windows

at hybrid cars whooshing soundlessly towards the shore
where bracelets of kelp wrap around the ankles
of Japanese fisherman, knee-deep in sea.

Gray whales breech in the channel;
Chumash bones rest high up
in the hills.

Regret

Only witchgrass iced hard between our houses.
All the signs not appearing: no dog asleep, stone skipped.
The curtain waxing then waning, the light shut off and silent.

Men outside my windows: the novillero drunk and begging,
the man in the street, calling out to ask if the cat is mine.
Others wanting in and through, palms pressed to cold glass.

How is it to surrender to the life you almost had? I almost
carried. Our histories laid flat like cards, our hands entwined.
Then slipped away: their heartbeats, my husband's chimney of a sigh.

Childhood Illness

Corn stalks. Cabinets spilling their words.
Pledges, prescriptions, bottles of pain relief.
The balloon let go. Silk husk of skirt folded,
put in a drawer. Everything that falls out.
Cotton balls: stacked clouds on the dresser.
Folded prayer, waxed wing, Gregorian chant.
Rustle through wind, through the flue.
The farm house, the orchard. Fruit dangling
like light bulbs in a narrow hallway. A pair
of tweezers, iodine. Leaves and chimneys.
Soot awaiting fire. Soot from fire. Suit left
to hang in fire. Smoke through the orchard,
swallows flee. Wings are colored tomes:
unbound, unflowered, unstringed. Over
the field— stained bandages torn free…

We Ease into this Life and Ease out; the Rest Is Struggle

I. Cognitive-neurological testing/ UCSF/October, 2012

Follow my fingers. Can you see them wiggle?
Can you push down on my hand gently?
Put your arms out like you're stopping traffic.
I'm going to tickle the bottom of your foot.
Where are we? Who is the President?
Please remember these five words.
I'll ask you what they are in a few minutes.
Face, velvet, church, daisy, red.
Now twist your wrists like your screwing in a light bulb.
Can you draw a clock with all the numbers in the right place?
My husband: "Face, clock. I can't remember the others."

II. IVF treatment/ Querétaro, Mexico/ November, 2012

I imagine sparks of life inside me: 1-2-3?
Not knowing if they are there or not,
if I am here or who
will remember the waiting to know.
In this moment
my hands are empty.
In the future they are holding theirs.

III. Regression to a past life/San Miguel de Allende,
Mexico/December, 2012

My body hangs heavy in his arms.
Then the memory of being dragged
across the cool stones of the river floor,
swept like debris by the current
and then his arms cradling my spine.
Though my body is unconscious,

I can see the villagers on the shore
outside the doors of their thatched huts,
under palms. They are waving, and then still.
I feel my body being released onto land.
I feel peace inside the glow, there
floating in my luminous star above them all:
the failed hero, the disbelieving crowds,
the unforgiving river.

Upright of Everything
    —after a sketch by Ken Morrow

I.

View out the night window:
crisscross of branch
beyond meeting
of glass and wood—
From the back of the room
to the back of the dark.

Silhouette of something
blocking. Further afield,
columns of light. Two
parallel signals calling
forth, hidden here—
backed in, wanting out.

II.

There is grass
on everything
and hair. Tangles
on air on bone
in the upright hall.
Dark furious scratches
on robes windows
telephone poles
then light coming through
at some instance
shone on splitting
opening standing
upright of everything
in the distance.

First Trimester

The baby robs me of fuel—a renegade youth siphoning gas
from an abandoned car—leaves me wheeling
in the shower, butterflies lodged behind my eyes.

But I go back to the swim, arms arched ahead of me
like the doorways of a temple,
my little thief sending up prayers through the waves.

Second Trimester: Central Park Playground in April

See the toddler in mango sneakers galloping like a horse;
little girls in fur collars riding pastel elephants on springs?
Haitian nannies stand by, suck their petal-white teeth.

Children in lime safety vests hold onto a single rope:
a Conga-line of neon bees. When they meld
with the swarm, teacher knows which are hers.

I've come to rehearse; my daughter kicks to please,
lets me know as I sit on a warm bench in weak sunshine,
that she's eager to test this lure of breeze.

Third Trimester: Dreaming During the Advent of Rain

My hands are spread over my womb,
my daughter displacing fluid
as she gravitates to the other side.

Then I'm in my mother's house,
the one I was born into, and it's dark.
On top of the dishes, figurines, antiques:

a snow of almond dust. But no mother,
only abandoned rooms and the eerie glow
of her pollen lacing still things.

I drive down the highway. Bruised clouds
hang over mountains, the valley.
A lone straw sombrero waits on the busy road.

The rains come. I visit a friend
who is moving into her new home.
We walk past bamboo in her garden

through swarms of flying ants run out
of their nests by water. In Mexico, this is
how we know the season has begun.

When I see the wrinkled sheets of her bed,
I know my mother has left for good.
Her labor: to scrape each almond by hand.

Soon, the drone of the ants' wings slow.
They begin turning up dead in piles.
The hat? Long ago blown away or flattened.

The rains will stop, my daughter be born:
another naked head peering into the autumn air.
In town, a woman sells scissors

she keeps locked in a glass case.

What the Morning Brings

Roses at the door, the ground purpled with rain.
I'm off with my husband to his doctor for tests,
while my daughter sleeps in another woman's arms.
Her tiny yellow socks mark the trail to daybreak.

A Family Goes to Bed: Ventura, CA

"The light was blocked, so I shifted some
alarm clocks," my husband says to explain
why he's moving around in bed.

On the dining room floor:
orange and green broccoli slaw
scattered in the moonlight like Easter hay.

C. humps me as she nurses, in tune
with Harley engines on the freeway.
John tosses like an old mastodon.

There is an accident report to file,
a prescription to fill, all our bones
shining in bed tonight as we prepare for sleep.

Parkinson's Disease

Alone when the horse is serious:
I have to consciously slow down.

He loved the silence.

What am I to do with so much sky?
A sigh what happens in the sky—

You toss the stars like clover seed,
your tongue that tongue you keep.

The road is too long for arriving home.
There is a field—I'll meet you there.

The dragging of his feet—

Geometric designs in simplicity:
the bare branch that branch made black.

Cento Bingo Sources: *Bucolics* by Maurice Manning; my translations of *Collectable Images (Imagenes Para Coleccionar)* by Mexican poet, Martha Favila; and *Who Let in the Sky, A son's tribute to his father: Goh Poh Seng's couragous struggle with Parkinson's Disease,* by Kagan Goh. Rumi.

A Quiet Life

My husband measures out puzzle pieces in his towering office,
nibbles on a single square of Mexican chocolate.
In the garden, under the loquat, our baby girl rocks on my chest.

Even so, I leave them daily to drive down the valley
into San Miguel. The view spools out, meeting the sun
as I turn down and round.

I note the weak link, not a turn out, but a thin,
dented aluminum rail lining the mountain's edge
on the curve of highway where the panorama goes wide.

Sometimes I dream, not that I am careening beyond the barrier
into the abyss—
but that I'm the woman in the house on the hillside below,

in warm sleep between husband and child
when the car falls through the old, make-shift roof
to land where our family still abides.

Late Summer Garden
    —after Ezra Pound/Li Po, "The River Merchant's Wife"

The paired butterflies are already yellow with August—
cymbal clash of wings, powder settling on braided weeds.

A black cloud sails over our roof
toward mountains, purple shadow
beaten between our bodies.

Light flits through bamboo reeds. The notes
of uncontrolled growth, dusted tiles, bellies full of rain.

A house without walls, the unwoven ties of a hammock.
Lingering clink of a mast's halyard,
the strings of a violin's bow unleashed upon us.

In the final moments of heat, water falls in musical sheets—
soft antennae search for gold between our fingers.

Wheeling

I want to tell you how it ended
that September afternoon,
with me running down Broadway,
in the opposite direction
to interview a babysitter,
baby strapped to my chest,
while my aunt and the Russian doorman
wheeled you in a burgundy office chair
the last block to safety.
Baby and I turned once
to watch the three of you
pass the cupcake shop and bank
around the corner…,
you, an actor wheeling off stage.
The things you see in New York!

I had walked you the two city blocks
before we got to 88th.
One inch at a time,
your whole body frozen up.
You clung to the scaffolding for life.
I stood half a block away as always,
beckoning you forward with my right hand,
holding our daughter
to my chest with the left.
I could have used a traffic cop's whistle.
Was there a way for her sake
to make your baby-steps look fun?

I had run to you, baby bouncing,
from my aunt's apartment
after the second phone call.
In the first, you said you were three blocks away
and would see us soon.
45 minutes later you were still three blocks away.

"I'm in trouble," you said,
and I knew what you meant.
I raced out the building with Caroline,
still half an hour before my appointment,
and waved at the doorman.
I'd get you home somehow.
Tell you later how it ended.

Fixed

There's a photo on my phone where I'm staring at the camera,
my two-year old is staring at the TV, and
my husband is staring into space.

We're lying on top of each other in a sandwich,
C. on top of me on top of John—
a toothpick of light running through our hearts.

The light holds us together in the moment,
carries us through hospitalizations,
separations, my daughter's first words yearning

into being,
her hand extended as she grows
to help her father walk.

We see the light, all three of us, in different places…
a heart monitor in the dark, a cartoon flickering
across a screen, a ghost in the window dressing.

My own eyes look back at me in the camera
to show me the way towards an unpredictable future.
Together we watch for signs, unmovable

and melded into one.

Sit

There are two chairs,
side by side against a wall,
and you should be in one of them.
I could sit in the other.

They would suit a Sicilian
man and wife.
Straight-backed,
Mediterranean blue.

We could hold hands or not,
or just let our shoulders touch.
Perhaps it would please the photographer to show our feet,
crossed at the ankles.

The chairs are empty now,
casting shadows on a wall.
Maybe a price tag dangles
from one of their painted slats.

I'm sure no one would mind
if we sat down.
If a photograph makes you nervous,
we could just be together for a while—

Breathe, smile and dream of that cobalt sea.

What You Said After Your Death

After you were gone you came to me and sat on the couch. You could walk and talk, and I thought maybe you had returned to thank me. You said you were leaving me.

"But you died," I wanted to say. "You can't leave me now."

Your pinkie fingertip rested just beside my knee and would leap up as you spoke.
"It's just no good anymore. We're broken," you insisted.

Your hands were younger than I remembered them, smooth like milky envelopes.

From where we sat, we were looking out through the open patio door onto the garden and the pepper tree. Behind the tree, the sky turned to orange powdered dusk.

Then the light was gone as hundreds of moths, each the size of your hand and the color of wet tobacco, flew in through the door and filled the house. They lit on our bodies and hair, the dining room table and Talavera vase filled with lavender.

You walked through the cloud of them out into the fading garden light and did not turn to say goodbye. I could hear the flapping of the moths' wings fill my throat.

Composing

It's a long walk to my compost heap, weeks before I pull on boots,
    stand heavy before the two piles.
        What comes up as I shovel one half

onto the other always surprises me: bottle caps, purple lace, foil
    from a tenant's barbeque.
        For three years now, plastic soldiers spring

out of nowhere. Whose child? What history, the pieces of wire,
    lemon rinds and dog bones,
        for someone

who doesn't have a dog, knows citrus is slow to decompose.
    The mountain spits up pieces of itself in rock,
        and who's building with these bricks?

I select and set aside nature's more permanent toys: cactus paddles,
    jacaranda pods and avocado pits,
        the silky husks of bamboo.

They return endlessly as I root through. I am not alone
    on this hill top: A hummingbird
        in the orange tree, the valley's echo

of drums. We throw it all in, despite advice,
    and it comes back
        black, expectant earth.

Spring Coming

My tambourine makes grasshoppers jump.
As a child I was afraid to climb trees.

I see the trunk now:

Cloud, cabbage, change.
A husband gone.

There is sap, amber bubbling.

Be specific in prayer:
I dreamt of snowflakes.

Like a red ball of fire
wanting to be seen,
wanting to be seen,
the dream rolls under my mother's skirt.

You don't know what you know.

The gypsy woman outside my window sings:
Orion, musk, fennel, linen.

There's a corncob in the agave and bells ringing everywhere…

Laura Juliet Wood, B.A. in Creative Writing from Hollins University and M.F.A. in Fiction from Columbia University, has lived in San Miguel de Allende, Mexico for twenty years. She and her three small children now divide their time between that colonial city and her hometown of Pensacola, Florida. She was widowed on May 4th, 2016, the day her newborn twins turned one month old.

Her poems have been featured in *Crab Creek Review, The Hollins Critic, The Los Angeles Review, Atlanta Review, Minerva Rising* and *West Marin Review* among many others. She most recently taught poetry workshops for The San Miguel Writers' Conference and at the Pensacola Cultural Center. She is author of the poetry chapbook *All Hands Lost* (Finishing Line Press, 2013).

Her translations of poetry and prose in Spanish have appeared in Mexico City's *The Ofi Press* and the first three volumes of *Solamente en San Miguel*. She is co-translator with Allen Josephs of *The Insistence of Harm* by Spanish poet Fernando Valverde (University Press of Florida, 2019).

www.ingramcontent.com/pod-product-compliance
Lightning Source LLC
LaVergne TN
LVHW041511070426
835507LV00012B/1492